ARCHITECTURE & DESIGN LIBRARY

AMERICAN COUNTRY

• ARCHITECTURE & DESIGN LIBRARY •

AMERICAN COUNTRY

Lisa Skolnik

©1998 by Michael Friedman Publishing Group, Inc.

ISBN 0-7607-5482-9

Color separations by Colourscan Overseas Co. Pte. Ltd.
Printed in China by C.S. Graphics Shanghai Co., Ltd.

1 3 5 7 9 10 8 6 4 2

To Marcia, and our past and future trips
in pursuit of stuff "extraordinaire."

Acknowledgments
Thank you to the staff at Michael Friedman Publishing Group,
particularly to my editors Francine Hornberger and Wendy Missan.

Contents

INTRODUCTION

What does a rough-hewn log cabin in Maine have in common with a pristine white Southern plantation house? Much more than meets the eye. The same holds true for a quaint Cape Cod cottage or tidy New England saltbox, lodgings that seem worlds apart from the squat adobes or low-slung Spanish colonials of the Southwest. Yet they are all kindred structures, for they are all part of the architectural vernacular that comprises American country style. This domain is undeniably as broad as the nation is big, embracing in its scope places to live and pieces to fill these places that are rustic and quaint, primitive and austere, or stately and poised.

American country encompasses elements from many different arenas because it represents all the diverse groups that settled this land. Each of these groups had different needs, different aesthetic legacies, and different skills, and their residences reflected these distinctions.

It was only natural for the first settlers to imbue their residences with elements that reflected their heritage. Thus, homes in the East tended to be based on forms familiar to that region's northern European settlers, such as the typical country cottages or farmhouses found throughout England, Germany, France, Holland, and Sweden. These designs eventually trickled farther west as the rest of the country was settled. At the same time, Native American and Mexican influences permeated the Southwest and made their way east. And what was inside each home followed suit: furnishings reflected the cultures and capabilities of furniture makers and artisans.

On the eastern seaboard, colonial quarters and accoutrements were heavily influenced by the English. The William and Mary, Queen Anne, Chippendale, Federal, and Empire periods were reinterpreted. Country craftsmen kept up with new woodworking techniques, though their creations tended to be simpler than that of their city counterparts: they often brought their own imaginative decorative additions to these designs. Thanks to these "amendments," rural styles that ran the gamut from rustic to ornate were born.

OPPOSITE: *A classic that came into vogue right after the American Revolution, this weatherboard Federal home has traditional details such as symmetrical six-over-six sash windows and a square-columned portico. The spread of this fashionable residential design in the last decades of the eighteenth century was related to newly arrived craftsmen from England.*

Similarly, the Germans and French who left Europe during the same period left their mark. The Germans, who for the most part settled outside Philadelphia, preserved their folk traditions with the same frothy, ornately embellished furniture they had left behind, while the major contribution of the French immigrants, who settled along the Mississippi River, was the armoire, a now-ubiquitous piece in any decor.

From religious communities such as the Quakers, Shakers, Amish, and Puritans, who settled in the Northeast and Midwest, came a form of country styling based on strong, clean-lined designs that were in keeping with the strict creeds that dictated their lifestyles. The homes and furnishings these groups produced were simple, plain, functional, and devoid of extraneous embellishments. Much of it is so straightforward and elegant that it is often emulated in minimalist designs today. Authentic pieces are coveted, and reproductions, especially of Shaker pieces, are routinely produced.

In the Southwest, design was influenced by Native American cultures and the Spanish conquistadors, who introduced metal hand tools to the continent in 1598 when they established the first permanent colony in New Mexico. Missionaries and Spanish *carpinteros* taught natives to build Spanish-style furniture and adobe dwellings. The missionaries also introduced the Spanish tradition of furnishing a home sparsely. In the mid-1800s, Anglo-American settlers started trickling into the area with their own design traditions. Today, these influences have developed into a distinct Southwestern style that combines elements from all three cultures.

R I G H T : *Most colonial homes were made of wood since it was more readily available, cheaper, and faster to build with than stone or brick, which were usually reserved for finer buildings. But German and Dutch settlers routinely built stone houses with low walls and deep roofs, such as this country cottage.*

ABOVE: *Barns, which came in many incarnations, were found flanking farmhouses as well as homes in smaller towns. Today they are often converted to residences, especially those that exist in more populated areas. Their rustic demeanor make them perfect candidates for creating a country-style residence.*

OPPOSITE: *Houses in the South were built with high ceilings, large windows, wide overhangs, and shaded porches to stave off the heat. They also had strict neoclassical decorative treatments, evident here in the Ionic columns on the portico. Porches based on classical temple portico forms were also quite popular on these homes, especially on those that anchored plantations, since they lent elegance and grandeur to a structure.*

Aside from cultural disparities, environment was perhaps the strongest factor to influence American shelters. Homes in the North and the heartland were designed to retain heat and withstand harsh elements, while those in warmer climates were devised with an emphasis on keeping cool. Hence a variety of well-insulated, cozy structures of wood, clay, stone, or brick punctuated with small, tightly fitted windows and large chimneys sprung up in the North, while homes in the South were built with high ceilings, large windows, porches, and courtyards.

And just as these structures and the effects that filled them were based on the heritages of their creators and on environmental considerations, they were also determined by the resources of the new land. Country craftsmen had to work with whatever materials were available in their locales, which usually meant indigenous wood, stone, and clay. This led to experimentation and alteration, resulting in a variety of new innovations and designs.

American country style was touched by social as well as historical influences. In the nineteenth century, both the Industrial Age and the Victorian mores affected this style. Thanks to the machine age, it took less time to make furniture and it was more affordable. But industrialization caused a backlash and created a nostalgic attraction to the preindustrial past. Decorating trends encompassed all sorts of furnishings that filled this calling, especially pieces that were rustic, romantic, eccentric, and sentimental, often made of exotic materials such as roots, branches, twigs, bark, and horn instead of wicker, cast iron, and wood.

Today, country style is not really about "the country" at all, but is, rather, a mind-set. It's comfortable, nurturing, and engaging—in essence, an alternative to hard-edged or sleekly orchestrated "urban" decors. And above all else, it's multifaceted. The style can be minimal and architectural, as the Shakers showed us with their pristinely crafted, spare interiors. Or it can be flooded with texture, color, and pattern, all cunningly employed to evoke moods that range from rustic and primitive to romantic and posh. In fact, the variety of elements and environments that qualify as country is nothing short of astonishing.

The humble hodgepodge is just as much a part of the milieu as the refined, carefully coordinated room. And provenance or purism are unimportant; tenor and spirit are far more significant to consider when creating a country interior than authenticity or period. Pieces can be reproductions or representative of different eras and styles; ultimately it is the mix and mood created with these accoutrements that counts.

The following chapters will show all the looks that comprise American country style and the many ways there are to achieve them. You can choose from a wide variety of furnishings, finishes, and surface treatments. And be creative when planning your design in this style—these ideas can be adapted to virtually any type of home.

ABOVE: *Door hoods were common in colonial times since they gave protection and decorative emphasis to an entry without the expense of a porch. Thanks to the addition of Doric columns, this hood has the aesthetic importance of a porch.*

OPPOSITE: *A one-room cabin was the typical home of a pioneer. Swedish settlers are thought to have introduced log construction to the colonies in the early eighteenth century, a method of building that became popular in rural areas. The cabins have small, tightly fitted windows and doors for protection from the elements.*

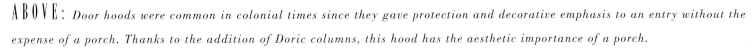

CHAPTER ONE

THE MIXING BOWL: DETAILS OF COUNTRY STYLE

Getting the details right is an essential part of creating a country home, be it cozy, quaint, primitive, or spare. And since the country interior has spanned the centuries in America, there's no need to stick to any specific period. The roots of the style come from our rural past when practical considerations rather than worries about beauty dictated the way a home looked. Elements that filled a country room were chosen for need, not want, and were rarely purist in ethic, so almost anything goes. Pieces from the colonial and Shaker periods are just as valid as Victorian- or Depression-era furnishings, and all of these pieces can be mixed at will in the American country interior.

Since there are no strict constraints about what works and what doesn't—and no rules and regulations to follow about what finishes, furniture, or fabrics constitute American country style—be creative. The materials that were employed to build a country abode, such as stone, brick, logs, and planks, are ideal for adorning the interior of a home and can be used on walls, ceilings, and floors. Pieces or effects from every era can be employed for furnishings. They can take the form of rough-hewn primitives, fancied-up antiques, or even contemporary pieces, as long as they are arrayed with a country sensibility.

OPPOSITE: *Simplicity can speak for itself, evoking a mood that's often impossible to achieve under other conditions. The austere bones of a room, especially if they incorporate architecturally significant details such as beams, sash windows, or paneled wood doors, can often stand alone with little accessorizing. A room can be transformed with a few powerful antique pieces, as in this example where a rustic bowl filled with woven fruit sits atop a gateleg table.*

Yet creating a country sensibility is perhaps the hardest part of the equation, for there are no hard-and-fast rules. Be aware of history and tradition, but don't follow them obsessively. Choose colors that have the earthy overtones exemplified by vegetable dyes and milk paints, but make sure they please you first rather than epitomize the style. Follow the same game plan with furnishings: pieces that fulfill your needs are more important than items that just look good. Finish it all off with decorative accessories that tie everything together or balance pieces from different periods. For instance, a contemporary cabinet can acquire a rustic ambience filled with a collection of primitive toys, and a group of framed samplers can give a plain plaster wall country appeal. Feel free to experiment, for trial and error is the best way to make it all work.

ABOVE: *There's power in numbers, as evidenced by these Shaker baskets, which make a much more powerful statement stacked in sets rather than displayed individually. Quilts folded atop the weathered blue hutch and draped in various places in the home further establish a country ambience.*

OPPOSITE: *A porch swing makes an unusual, eye-catching perch in the corner of a family room, giving the place solid originality. The house lacked a porch and the owners hit upon this solution so that they could swing their young children while reading. The "anything goes" spirit of American country style really comes across in this addition.*

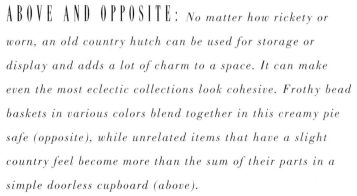

ABOVE AND OPPOSITE: *No matter how rickety or worn, an old country hutch can be used for storage or display and adds a lot of charm to a space. It can make even the most eclectic collections look cohesive. Frothy bead baskets in various colors blend together in this creamy pie safe (opposite), while unrelated items that have a slight country feel become more than the sum of their parts in a simple doorless cupboard (above).*

ABOVE: *The weathered front doors are the best attributes of this ancient hutch, so they've been left intact while the bottom doors have been removed to showcase collectibles such as decorative candlesticks, a tray handpainted with flowers, and a set of urns. Yet with still more to show, it makes good sense to use the top as a ledge for pitchers and teapots.*

ABOVE AND OPPOSITE: *The art of the tableau is just as much a part of country design as it is in any other style and can take many forms. Items may be different variations on a theme, such as these stars, which have been carefully arranged by color and scale to create an eye-catching display (above). Or they can be disparate and unique (opposite), combining elements both humble and grand unified by a carefully wrought balancing act to catch the eye and convey a country sensibility.*

ABOVE AND OPPOSITE: *Another way to highlight a tableau and imbue it with warmth is to anchor it with a source of light. The glow this light sheds on a setting will embrace everything it touches, and forges groupings of objects into cohesive vignettes. The burnished hues of antique woods come alive with illumination from a small table lamp, above, while opposite, collectibles on a worn, unfinished table are dramatically backlit against a window.*

ABOVE: *Every nook and cranny can be made interesting in a country home. Here, a porch is treated as grandly as a parlor with a picture hung right onto the home's exterior clapboard walls. All sorts of odd pieces come together here such as corn husks, a straw chair, and a wooden box filled with vegetables from the morning's stroll through the garden.*

BELOW: *A stairway goes from extremely worn to delightfully weathered with the addition of some well-chosen country collectibles. The pottery adds an earthy flavor while bright "watermelons" bring it all to life.*

ABOVE: *Upholstered armchairs were very rare in country homes because they were so expensive (their fabric was costly and they required the work of special tradesmen to make the frames and upholster them). But this cozy version looks right at home in a rough-hewn environment—proof that it's possible to hit just the right note between primitive and plush.*

ABOVE: *The rocking chair, one of the most familiar forms of seating in any home, happens to be an all-American innovation, with the first known examples dating from the 1750s. Just its presence provides an ample dose of country styling to its environment, not to mention comfort.*

ABOVE: *A rustic tableau takes on entirely new dimensions in this room awash in primary colors. Only a few appropriately colored accessories are necessary. The rag rug is purposely low-key to offset the room's vivid hues.*

CHAPTER TWO

THE KEEPING ROOM: ONE GREAT ROOM

The early American country home consisted of little more that just one room, for resources—be they manpower or materials—were scarce. This room was officially called the "keeping room," and all the activities of a household, from cooking and eating to gathering and sleeping, occurred here.

Homes were humbly built out of necessity, but there was also a great deal of historical precedence for this simple floor plan. Provincial shelters in Europe had consisted of only one or two rooms. When the Industrial Age brought prosperity to such rural areas, the sizes of homes started to increase. The keeping room became less utilitarian as kitchens, storage areas, and bedrooms were added onto homes. This room ultimately vanished as separate living and dining rooms came into vogue.

Today, the custom of a country-style keeping room has come full circle, for a large, open space that blends meeting and eating areas is once again a popular component of the contemporary residence. In its current incarnation, the keeping room is known as the "great room." Yet the resurgence of this singular space couldn't be more paradoxical, since the prosperity that initially fostered larger residences with more rooms, and also begot today's hectic lifestyles, spurred the development of this latter-day keeping room. For like its forerunner, this space fosters the sort of intimacy and togetherness we crave today. And though it harks back to the keeping room, it is a thoroughly modern response to contemporary life; it is primarily designed to comfort us.

In light of such a calling, it's easy to understand why the great rooms of today are often arrayed with country trappings. We want them to attract and soothe us and we use wiles of the style such as ambient fires, cozy furnishings, and rustic structural materials to make us feel snug and secure. Fires call for mammoth hearths or earthy fireplaces that add warmth and soul to a room; cozy furnishings keep the space comfortable; and rustic materials such as muscular log beams, burnished wood paneling, weathered planks, or mottled bricks give the room character and depth.

OPPOSITE: *Decorative woodwork that is loaded with elegance and intricacies has its place in a country context, but is ultimately quite different in spirit from its urban brethren. Here a complex system of intersecting beams that is also carried over to the ceiling and walls of the room offers much more than mere structural support to the space. It feels rustic in tone, but is actually quite elaborate and creates a sophisticated system of wainscotting on the walls.*

Given the fact that these spaces combine several functions and the square footage of two rooms, they can also incorporate dramatic architectural or decorative devices, such as soaring ceilings or intricate millwork. Clad in country "garb," such as knotty plank paneling or gnarled log beams, or filled with country furnishings and collectibles, the great room ranges from relatively routine to remarkable. Thanks to all these options, the great rooms of today are usually all-encompassing spaces that have universal appeal.

BELOW: *A great room in a contemporary home gets its country pedigree from its trappings. Its enormous size is made cozy and warm with wood and stone. Furnishings play off the tones of these surface treatments. The burnished caramel of the pine paneling and cool blue-grays of the hearth are echoed in the room's upholstered pieces, which are prominent enough to fill the space yet grounded in simplicity. Octagonal porthole windows and a collection of vintage tools break the monotony of the expansive walls.*

RIGHT: *Architecture and materials— namely the wide-open plan crowned with a soaring ceiling and the stone hearth paired with rough-hewn log beams and walls—give this space its country legacy. The mood and spirit created by these devices is so strong that the actual process of decorating becomes less significant, as evidenced by the eclectic pieces used here. The Arts and Crafts table and rocker, an Oriental carpet, and a Queen Anne chair assume a rustic spirit.*

LEFT: *Even when designed in warm country materials such as wood and stone, contemporary great rooms can seem sterile and cold due to their vast ceilings. In this room, a network of inter-secting rafters cuts the space down to more intimate proportions. It also serves to make the space far more interesting, since the wide-open expanse affords architects great creative leeway to devise structures that are "works of art" in themselves.*

RIGHT: *Nothing says "country" like a mammoth stone hearth and rough-hewn log walls and beams. The warmth and texture these elements dispense make them ideal components of an oversize room. They can make soaring spaces intimate as well as imbue them with country character, for virtually any decor can assume a quaint demeanor with these basics for a backdrop. And set against these architectural elements, pieces that are not necessarily country in pedigree, such as the deco-inspired furnishings here, can still seem pleasingly rustic.*

ABOVE: *Country styling can be rugged and elegant at the same time. Here, a craggy "physique" is outfitted in fine "garb," illustrating the point. The hearth and gables are clad in rough-hewn stone, and the rafters and cornices are crafted of coarsely cut beams. The gleaming floor and burnished furnishings are traditional and refined rather than rustic, though the room retains a country flavor thanks to its underpinnings.*

ABOVE: *British "club" style meets American country in this great room, where precisely tailored furnishings in paisleys and plaids are made less prim by weathered pine walls and coarse flagstone floors (as seen at left). The room also maintains a more formal mood, as the entertainment area is set off from the dining area by a sisal rug in buttery beige.*

ABOVE: *Although this vast great room has ample space for country collectibles, these pieces could easily become clutter if not presented properly. Quirky chairs are pegged to walls and kitschy odds and ends are set on the rafters to free up floor space and keep the room in order. Since wall space is at a premium, large, flat items, such as a caroms board and an advertising sign, are propped up against other pieces of furniture.*

ABOVE: *The inveterate collector who can't resist snapping up country artifacts can work a variety of them into the same environment with careful planning. Here, walls are kept pure white; sofas and chairs are covered in black and white checks or pinstripes; other furnishings are similar in hue; and like objects are tightly grouped together. Despite a profusion of pieces, everything blends together harmoniously.*

ABOVE: *There is no such thing as an authentic country-style sofa since upholstered furniture was rare in actual provincial residences (special craftsmen had to make them and woven fabrics were scarce). While the "shabby chic" or "colonial" styles have come to epitomize a country sensibility, there are other options. A boldly graphic quilt can turn any sofa into the star of the room, regardless of its style, as shown by the example above.*

LEFT: *Though great rooms tend to be more informal than separate living and dining areas, they can borrow a bit from both. In this version, well-edited country furnishings that are predominately Shaker in tone make the space at once casual and stately. A singular truss in the middle of the room is an architectural double entendre, paying homage to the traditional beamed country ceiling and setting up a subtle divider that still allows the room to function as one great space.*

RIGHT: *Thanks to multipurpose furnishings, the great room of this vintage cottage is exceptionally versatile. A chair-table tilts down to accommodate meals and can be moved away to be replaced by seating around the hearth. Though the chairs around the table are mismatched, they achieve a sense of unity because they all have box stretchers. Coincidentally, the chair-table sports the same design.*

LEFT: *A contemporary space gets a healthy dose of country styling with simple tongue-and-groove paneling and a stone chimney stack rising from an earthy hearth. Neutral upholstered pieces with high comfort quotients but no particular pedigree are joined with a rustic pine table and Native American rug to beef up the country ambience of the space.*

RIGHT: *Many
wood-burning stoves
do double duty: they
provide heat and
act as cookers. This
stove anchors a true
keeping room that
supports many
essential household
functions. A conver-
sation area in front
of the stove has a
low-slung table that
can also be used for
eating, while counters
and a butcher block
remain ready for
culinary tasks.*

ABOVE: *When one room comprises the bulk of a cottage, it's important to make it engaging and versatile. Slipcovers are a quick, easy, and economical way to do so, and better yet, they don't have to be perfect to ply their charms. Sheets, textiles, or lengths of interesting fabric can work as well as, or better than, custom-made versions. Here, chunky upholstered pieces are transformed from ordinary to enchanting and inviting with simply draped sheets pulled over the frames in just the right way. Plump pillows make comfortable, cozy accents.*

ABOVE: *These wooden cabinets in disparate hues have been weathered to the same dull glow, coordinating with the room's plank walls and forging the perfect backdrop for the vivid fabrics. Though the fabric patterns don't match, they work well together because each one relates to a hue already employed on the cabinets. But the tableau isn't set in stone: two of the pieces (the chair and coffee table at right) are actually draped with sheets that can be changed at will.*

CHAPTER THREE
ROOMS FOR LIVING: SEPARATE BUT EQUAL

O nce luxuries confined to homes in affluent cities, living and dining rooms are now very much a part of country homes. The true rustic cottage, which was built with just one or two rooms, acquired such formalities as it enlarged over the years. What was once the keeping room or kitchen became a living or dining room, which accounts for the massive hearths or brawny beams that grace many of these spaces. Newer homes, built in or since the nineteenth century, had separate living and dining rooms as prosperity spread to all reaches of the United States.

In the homes of today, country styling can be easily adapted to both of these rooms. And architectural provenance is relatively unimportant. Although it's nice to have burnished paneling, gnarled beams, rugged plank floors, or sash windows, a country mood can often be evoked, or teased out, with the right furnishings. Sometimes all it takes is one great piece, such as a rustic cupboard or a weathered harvest table. Often, country style can be achieved through a decorative paint treatment, folksy fabrics, or displays that show off whole collections of country artifacts.

Ultimately, though, the living or dining room that embraces country style strives to offer a cozy, homey environment that sets its occupants at ease. The living room is a space for relaxing with family or meeting with friends, while the dining room is at its best filled with guests sharing delicious food and lively, meaningful discourse. Given this calling, comfort and ease come first and dictate much.

Functional yet comfortable furnishings that aren't necessarily historical but elicit the right ambience are the most important elements of these spaces, such as cushy upholstered sofas and chairs, and large sturdy armoires for hiding contemporary electronic equipment in the

OPPOSITE: *A chair-table affords a room the utmost in versatility. Here it allows maximum use of a handsome hearth, permitting different activities to transpire in front of the fire. When open, it creates a formal dining environment, and when closed it can be moved to one side so the sofa and chairs can be pulled up to create a conversation area.*

living room and generous wood tables ringed with comfortable chairs in the dining room. Yet, it is often impossible to get authentic country pieces that possess these attributes because the necessary resources and skills weren't available in rural areas, and even when they were, they were on a far smaller scale than the pieces of today. The same holds true for the classic cupboard or armoire, which could never accommodate today's electronic equipment.

Hence these rooms can be filled with a wide range of furnishings, be it original or reproduction. The success of these spaces depends more on the careful blending of the formal and casual than anything else. Living rooms can easily incorporate new upholstery, just as dining rooms can be outfitted with a wide range of dining sets that will do the job. It's the overall environment these pieces help develop that is most important, and it can often be fostered by the way a room is arrayed with accessories. These are rooms to be lived in and enjoyed every day—not just on special occasions.

LEFT: *A contemporary space is graced with country flavor by the elements of its decor. A slim wood mantelpiece accentuates a small gas-flame fireplace, while a black-and-yellow brick pattern gives a folksy flavor to modern narrow moldings. Furnishings follow suit, with a mismatched rustic wood dining set; chairs and a sofa covered in a splashy floral print that evoke the sense of a cottage garden; and a wool dhurrie with a floral motif.*

LEFT: *Chairs of three periods (from left to right) Queen Anne, William and Mary, and Chippendale, hold court around a William and Mary coffee table and are given a unified demeanor by their dark wood frames and an Oriental carpet that defines the sitting area. The doors, door frames, and mantel are painted in soft shades of green to offset plain white walls and to make the space more inviting.*

RIGHT: *Wedgwood blue is hardly the color one would expect to see applied to paneling and rustic beams, yet it polishes this living room to perfection. The chalky finish imbues the paneled wall with a provincial overtone and plays off other elements in the room, such as the upholstery fabric, curtains, cupboard, and worn floor with its residue of blue pigment.*

ABOVE: *In true colonial form (for the term applies to a time frame that spans almost two centuries), this room blends pieces from several periods together. A Chippendale chair hovers in the corner; a contemporary Queen Anne sofa with charming stitched pillows skirts a wall; and reproduction benches, stools, a chest, and a cupboard that all pay homage to Shaker style fill the rest of the space. A true country feel is achieved, since the furniture as well as the accessories evoke a homespun early American mood.*

ABOVE: *The essential ingredients for a classic American country room are all here—a plump sit-and-sink easy chair, a well-worn leather sofa, a distressed wood coffee table, a painting of a rustic landscape, and wood paneled walls painted a dark green. Each of the elements alone may not necessarily say "country," but together, they create an effect of a refuge from a fast-paced life for the residents.*

RIGHT: *During the Federal period, walls of the finest rooms were papered with elegant scenery for those who could afford it. Preserved to this day, the picturesque paper imparts a quaint warmth instead of regal splendor on the living room. Curvy Queen Anne chairs upholstered with a flamboyant floral fabric are elegant, yet enhance the warm feel of the space and serve to soften the room's neoclassical elements.*

LEFT: *There's no need for purism to create a country demeanor: the style takes sustenance from imagination and daring. Here, a contemporary leather sofa, French fauteuils, an Empire cabinet, and a pie safe and wall hutch with true rustic pedigree set the stage for what could be a more formal space. But blooms rather than brocades cover the chairs, matching pillows transform the nature of the sofa, and the lush floral patterns of a huge hooked rug and valances give the space country styling.*

ABOVE: *Mini prints are particularly well suited to country homes, especially since their popularity stems from the very early days of printed wallpapers and fabrics in the eighteenth century. Here, a collection of small iron bells and kitchen and garden tools mixes particularly well with an intensely hued mini print, for both are equally dark and diminutive. Using the print on only some of the walls keeps the room from becoming too busy.*

ABOVE: *Windows everywhere keep the materials and hues of this room from feeling overpowering. Left beautifully bare, they let light spill into the room and bring the warm tones of the furnishings and finishes to life. There's clearly no need for window treatments in this rustic space as nature provides privacy as well as a verdant backdrop that tames the room's design.*

LEFT: *Wallpaper and paint can fill a room with style at a reasonable expense. A moss green wallpaper with a charming floral print, a clean white dado and molding on the walls, and a black-and-white check painted floor infuses this room with energy. Refined wood dining pieces in rich mahogany get a dose of country styling through these decorative devices.*

ABOVE: *Even polished furnishings, such as an intricately carved Victorian dining table and refined Viennese chairs, can acquire a country flavor. Here, a Depression-era hooked rug that sports a log cabin motif sets a distinctly country tone while other American country artifacts, such as art pottery with mellow brushed glazes and an antique Federal chandelier, strengthen the effect.*

OPPOSITE: *Chair-tables made sense in colonial times because residences were comprised of only one or two rooms that had to be multifunctional. But in a traditional dining room, the tabletop no longer has to be folded up when not in use—unless the owners want it that way. This type of table also presents an unusual dining surface, since a round shape is egalitarian and not common in rustic pieces.*

ABOVE AND RIGHT: *As these two distinctive yet similar spaces show, the same pickings can create a different presence in a room. The basic ingredients of these dining rooms are exactly the same—worn plank floors, six-over-six sash windows surrounded by plain wooden casements, colonial candlestick-style chandeliers, harvest tables, and Windsor chairs—but the result is far from the same. The stark lines of the comb-back Windsor chairs joined with strong terra-cotta walls and prominent contemporary art make one room (above) seem Shaker-spare and modern. But conventional creamy walls combined with traditional art, softer bow-back Windsors, a colonial sideboard, and a decorated fireplace and chimney stack create a warmer, more conventional feel (right).*

LEFT: *The sort of massive logs usually found in larger structures give this dining room—where bold trappings are employed in an unusually well-balanced way— lodge-style grandeur. Equally massive furnishings made of logs, planks, and tree limbs, which are in keeping with the Adirondack style of the room, complete the rustic picture.*

LEFT: *Two sides of country styling are revealed in this dining room where rustic meets refined. Dichotomous elements are paired together to stunning effect, such as gnarled log walls chinked with coarse plaster and polished pine panels crossed with an asymmetric design. Spare Shaker-flavored pieces that play to both the primitive and contemporary aspects of the room round out the setting and imbue it with timeless elegance.*

RIGHT: *Restraint keeps the pieces in this room from overwhelming each other. Almost everything is tucked away behind closed doors in the stenciled cupboard; the gleaming table is bare save for a fruit-laden basket centerpiece; textiles are kept simple with pinstripe chair cushions and modest gingham window treatments; and the walls are left mostly bare. A predominantly brick-red Oriental carpet plays off similar tones in the burnished furnishings and ties the elements of the decor together.*

LEFT: *Coarse plank and plaster walls are softened with sheer lace curtains, which add an aura of refinement and allow diffused light to stream into the dark room. While it would be difficult to adorn these walls with pictures, they are the perfect backdrop for storing kitchen implements such as baskets, pitchers, pans, ladles, and coffee mugs. Mix-and-match furnishings also work particularly well in this rough-hewn milieu. A rag rug is the perfect finishing touch.*

RIGHT: *A few well-placed, polished accessories can go a long way toward dressing up a rugged room, as shown here. Blue-and-white china plates grace a gnarled beam that serves as a mantel, and delicate creamy bowls and glass pieces adorn a wood table. A refined piece of art pottery filled with flowers makes for a lovely centerpiece and becomes the center of attention in the room.*

ABOVE: *A huge collection of printed Staffordshire china is shelved and hung on walls to show it off to fine effect. Boldly striped walls in a soft blue and cream harmonize with the blues found in most of the dishes, setting the collection off to perfection. An overflow of dishes tops a rustic sideboard, adding further dimension to the room by giving it a cozy Victorian tenor.*

CHAPTER FOUR

COUNTRY KITCHENS:
THE HEART OF THE HOME

The time-honored country kitchen has long been acknowledged as the heart of a home, and therefore, it should capture warmth, family life, and hospitality within its confines. This ambience can be easily achieved with earthy, humble materials that serve to counterbalance the sleek kitchen equipment available today.

With its charm and warmth, the country kitchen is the perfect antidote for our everyday chaotic lives. And the American country kitchen decor can be adapted to a wide range of tastes. It can be rustic and cottage-quaint or simple with rough-hewn splendor. Or, it may be fine-tuned to one of the many styles covered under the American country umbrella, such as Early American, Shaker, Adirondack, or Southwest.

But perhaps the main reason why country kitchens are coveted today and show up in so many residences is because of their practicality. In addition to the relaxed atmosphere these rooms exude, the materials used to achieve the look are hardy, economical, and utilitarian. Prosaic elements such as wood, brick, stone, or tile reign supreme and are cost-efficient, relatively indestructible, easy to clean, and only improve with age.

The country kitchen doesn't even necessarily have to be rustic, for the sensibility can be adapted to an urban or contemporary setting. Earthy materials can be blended with elements of high-tech or ultramodern design, adding warmth, balance, and intrigue to the room.

OPPOSITE: *A variety of rugged woods is often employed in country kitchens, since the woods will create an unpretentious and informal ambience. Here, a medley of woods, all worn with age and use, is responsible for the character, warmth, and appeal of the space. Other accents in this room that give the space its country appeal are baskets and pots hanging from the rafters and a quaint iron stove.*

Steel counters can top wood cabinets; open-wood shelving can hold the usual kitchen accoutrements and make a sleek environment inviting; and brick or tile can be installed on plain walls to provide them with depth and texture.

Thanks to such versatility, virtually any kitchen can get a healthy dose of country styling. Show off country collectibles or decorative accessories; furnish the space with rustic, primitive, or colonial pieces; introduce motifs with fabrics, tile, and color; or use surface treatments with paints or stains to modify floors, cabinets, and walls. If you're lucky enough to be starting from scratch, pave floors with planks, brick, or stone; craft cabinets out of wood; clad walls in logs, stone, or tile; and finish off the ceiling with an intricate and interesting support system made of beams or logs.

The country kitchen has come a long way from the keeping room. Thanks to the creativity and ingenuity we pour into the space, today it has become a "great room" in itself, for no other style of kitchen can be as inviting, flexible, utilitarian, and engaging all at the same time.

ABOVE: *British cottage styling comes to America with a crafty twist, for the traditional millwork in this kitchen gets a few modifications that pay homage to the eclecticism of this country. For instance, rail-and-stile cabinet doors have an updated decorative ring around their pulls, while open shelves are fitted with wicker baskets.*

RIGHT: *Hearths for heating and cooking were once the heart of every country home, but wood stoves assumed the same responsibilities much more efficiently in the nineteenth century. This iron stove is a secondary source of heat, but the image it conjures up is a primary design statement that's powerful enough to steep the whole room in country imagery.*

ABOVE: *Wood and brick may evoke the sense of a traditional country kitchen, but this space is anything but old-fashioned. Though the hearth seems primal, it's topped with a sleekly refined copper-clad flue that matches a state-of-the-art exhaust system, giving it an air of sophistication. The whole setup extends across a lineup of several high-tech appliances, which are creatively housed in rustic woods and gleaming black granite. The unusual blend of materials makes for a stunning and serviceable space.*

ABOVE: *A large kitchen in a new home gets its old-fashioned flavor from Shaker-style cabinets and sash windows with small panes. Rugged beams hung with herbs and dried flowers cut the space down to more intimate proportions. Classic country accents such as a blue-and-white plaid tablecloth, ruffled valances, a braided rag rug, dried-flower centerpieces in wood-carved "baskets," a candle-style chandelier, and a painted step stool round out the decor.*

ABOVE: *Too much of a good thing can be boring, which is why some of the wood cabinets in this kitchen have been painted a deep shade of green. Yellow ceramics play off a similar hue in the wood of the center island, while iron pans hung over the island complement the green paint. The result is a carefully contrived color scheme, which is highlighted with hooked rugs in similar hues.*

LEFT: *An element of surprise can shake things up a bit for the better. Here, a black-and-white checked tile floor, the epitome of urban chic, seems totally out of character with the country trappings in the space, yet it makes the room great by subtly playing off other elements of the decor: mellow two-tone wood cabinets; an antique pine cricket table with the same color value as the tiles; and decidedly rustic open-air shelves laden with crockery to counteract the urban influence of the floor.*

RIGHT: *Rustic trappings can coexist with high-tech appliances and soften the cold efficiency such equipment typically exudes. Here, a restaurant range is tempered by a sandy-toned tile backsplash, a stippled hood, and knotty pine cabinets that surround it. The refrigerator is cleverly masked behind a knotty pine façade.*

LEFT: *A few pieces of Quimper earthenware hanging on the back wall of this kitchen prove that a collection doesn't have to be massive to make a statement. All-white walls and a sweet lace liner on the ledge set them off. An old-fashioned range adds a sense of history, while the counter, made up of ceramic tiles hand-painted with flowers, has its own brand of country charm.*

LEFT: *A humble cottage kitchen goes from humdrum to exciting with a coat of barn red paint on its slat wood walls. The colored expanse lends country verve to the space, while an array of rustic trappings dots the area and garners it even more attention. Since the wood walls are one of the kitchen's strengths, it makes sense to highlight them. A twig bouquet and a hanging basket of corn, along with other country touches like a collection of teacups atop the molding around the door are perfect accents. Displaying utensils directly on the wall also makes the tiny area, which is very short on counter space, far more functional.*

ABOVE: *Simple wood shelves that span a wall organize oodles of dishes, glassware, and assorted odds and ends, but the turquoise cabinets below set them off to perfection. The secret to the success of this display is the sophisticated palette, for all the objects sport similar—and neutral—color values. The vivid hue of the cabinets draws the eye to the wall and brings the earth tones to life. Country collectibles on the unit's top shelf complete the setting.*

ABOVE: *An assortment of country accessories is unified through a carefully considered use of color on the cabinets and in the accessories themselves. If the wood cabinets were left unpainted, the kitchen may have been drab, but the combination of the earthy tones in the mixing and serving bowls above the cabinets and the muted pea green that covers the cabinets gives the room character and contrast.*

ABOVE: *It doesn't take much to dress up humble materials. Here, a deep shade of aquamarine paint calls verdant meadows to mind and gives finesse to plain plywood cabinets. A gingham valance and table runner, a gingham-and-floral swag, a tin filigree candle-style lighting fixture, a country-cute wallpaper border of apples applied at molding height, and a tile backsplash dressed up with hand-painted herbs give the kitchen a heavy dose of pretty provincialism.*

ABOVE: *A modest collection of blue-and-white transfer-printed china goes a long way in this kitchen, imbuing the room with loads of country charm. A stippled wall that mimics spatterware strengthens the mood, along with a frilly Victorian dining set, a snazzy black-and-white tablecloth, a wood spice rack, and a bucolic still life.*

LEFT: *Vintage stoves aren't specifically country in origin, but they do exude an old-fashioned aura that makes a great base in a country decor. Just a few true country trappings, such as a rack overflowing with well-worn pots, beadboard walls, and a quaint red-and-white table runner and rag-edged napkins over a brightly polished table strengthen the ambience but don't compete with the stove—a showstopper in its own right.*

RIGHT: *Long before there was refrigeration, baked goods were set to cool and stored in wooden-framed pie safes with elaborately patterned pierced-tin panels. Today, these are the kind of collector's pieces that can imbue a whole room with country charm. Here, just mimicking the coveted piece with a "pierced" refrigerator panel is enough to give the whole kitchen a country tone, as well as an ingenious way to diminish the impact of this huge modern appliance.*

LEFT AND ABOVE: *An eating area or breakfast nook off the main kitchen makes a perfect place to show off country collectibles. Stack rustic boxes on a sideboard, hang baskets from nails at the opening of the space, or take the door off a rustic cupboard to show off the contents, as shown at left. Or take one item and make it the center of attention. A bunch of country-cute tablecloths are layered on the table in the nook (above), while others were used to make cushions and upholster the fifties-era chairs.*

ABOVE: *The ultrarustic Adirondack log cabins and furnishings weren't part of the original country milieu, but were inspired as a reaction to growing urbanization in the nineteenth century. Designers created intricate homes and furnishings out of bent boughs, roots, branches, and twigs. Here, a dining set in the Adirondack vein teams up with a colorful diamond-patterned window border to liven up the spare eating area of a pure white beadboard kitchen.*

CHAPTER FIVE

BEDROOMS:
REFUGE FROM THE WORLD

At one time, rural families slept en masse in one room, which was also used for other activities such as eating, cooking, and entertaining. As America became more industrialized and our homes became larger, the country bedroom was born. If anything, it quickly became the most secluded spot in the home, for with the exception of this room, country-style homes usually feature open, communal, and multipurpose spaces geared to whole families. But whatever the country bedroom is furnished with, it follows one principle: it is not grand. This is a room where comfort comes first and governs every other consideration.

Not only is the country bedroom a haven today, it has retained many of the trappings from its first incarnation. For instance, the country bedroom may still feature a four-poster bed, which was originally draped on all sides for protection from the cold as well as privacy in communal environments. Huge storage cabinets or large blanket boxes also grace country bedrooms, holding spillover clothes and the like. Quilts that were often piled up to be used for warmth also have their place in the country bedrooms—and not just on beds. These quilts have proven to be the single most identifying mark of country style, often imbuing a whole room with warmth and rustic ambience, whether draped over a chair or hanging on a wall behind the bed's headboard.

OPPOSITE: *No item epitomizes the notion of American country styling better than the quilt. Given both the pedigree and appearance of this textile, which was begot by industrious and thrifty colonists who pieced together scraps of fabric in graphically imaginative patterns, its prominence as the premier country artifact makes sense. Introducing just one or a collection of many into a room will imbue the space with rustic ambience. It also counters the simplicity of spare country furnishings, bringing color and pattern to a relatively plain room.*

The country bedroom's four-poster bed can range from Shaker-spare to overtly ornamental and may or may not include a canopy. But these beds are rarely draped in full regalia today since drafts are controlled by central heating systems. Beds may be made of wood or metals that embrace a country sensibility such as brass or painted iron. Although the style of the bed sets a tone, dressing it to perfection may be the most critical aspect of furnishing a bedroom. This task not only makes the bed comfortable, but it gives the bed the allure needed to anchor the room. Making the country bed inviting and comfortable is often as easy as piling on plump pillows, thick quilts, and layers of crisp linens, all finished off with dusters and shams.

Storage is another important aspect of the country bedroom, and again the options are endless and easy to implement. Mammoth armoires and cupboards traditionally housed all of the effects of a household, but today they have become a staple in the country bedroom. They are coveted as much for their looks as their cubic footage, for they come in many varieties and are easy to find since antiques and reproductions of these pieces are plentiful. Dressers and chests are also available in old and new versions, and are often employed when the scale of a space prohibits larger pieces.

Given the flexibility and the endless options that can be explored for meeting storage and comfort needs, American country is a pragmatic, engaging, and easy style to employ in the bedroom.

ABOVE: *Country residents embellished their walls, floors, and furnishings with a wide range of designs by using stencils. Today these go a long way toward bringing a country demeanor to a room. Although sheer lace curtains, striped and floral wallpaper, and a wedding ring quilt contribute to the country charm in this space, the exquisite patterns on the bureau and bed are what imbue the room with true country styling.*

OPPOSITE: *A crocheted net covering draped across the curved canopy of this four-poster bed makes the perfect foil considering the large and dramatic nature of the piece. It not only coordinates particularly well with all the different textiles in the room, which include an all-white overshot coverlet, a calico patchwork quilt, a hooked wool rug, and sheer drapes, it doesn't fight the bold floral pattern on the wall.*

ABOVE: *Hand-loomed overshot coverlets are uniquely American, having originated in the eastern part of the United States in the eighteenth century. Originally made by women, these reversible textiles were eventually woven by professional male craftsmen who worked on looms they carried across the country. Overshots feature soft, heavy weft threads woven through a lighter background, in earthy shades of indigo blue, madder red, brown, and tan, and finishing touches such as elaborate borders or fringe are highly coveted in these textiles. Like quilts, they raise the country quotient of a room on their own, although they truly shine when paired with pieces in the same vein. This country bedroom that is purist in every sense is graced by a coverlet in primary colors that is complemented by colorful hooked carpets.*

RIGHT: *A cozy country bedroom makes the perfect retreat to be enjoyed at any time of day. The layout employed in this room creates two distinct activity areas: one for sleeping and the other for writing and reading. The chaise longue is perfectly positioned to take advantage of the room's inherent attributes, namely two windows that let natural light stream into the space. Hooked rugs with vibrant country themes separate the two distinct areas and make the open expanse the center of attention.*

RIGHT: *Antique wood pieces that derive great cachet from their authenticity are the focus of this small bedroom. A muted bed quilt, a rag rug, and a quilt suspended from a weathered green shelf that holds country collectibles punctuate the mellow brown tones of the furniture with texture and color, and help to brighten the room. A converted lantern is now a fixture, which contributes another dimension to the authenticity of the room.*

LEFT: *A hodgepodge of antique pieces, such as a colonial bed, an Empire chest of drawers, and a Shaker trunk, complement more rustic elements like a log cabin quilt and the room's rugged wood walls. The whitewashed plaster chinking between the wood planks plays off the creamy tones that dominate the quilt, and accessories have been kept to a minimum as the furnishings themselves are a bit bulky.*

RIGHT: *Quilts don't have to be confined to a bed or a wall. In this attic bedroom, a large collection of these and other textiles is displayed on the banister of a stairway, providing privacy as well as beauty. The plain rails go from utilitarian to ornamental, and the whole space takes sustenance from the texture and color of the quilts. And no detail has been overlooked: even the trundle is covered with a quilt.*

ABOVE: *Four-poster canopy beds originally had heavy drapes on all sides to both protect occupants from drafts at night and to provide privacy. But today, dressed in appropriate linens, they represent romantic country style at its best. It is important to outfit them in just the right way. Here, a bleached muslin canopy strikes just the right balance with the other elements of the room, which range from a daintily appliquéd quilt to densely patterned wallpaper.*

ABOVE: *Rag rugs, gingham curtains, and a pure white dust ruffle on a bed are the perfect neutrals to let rare finds, such as an intricate blue-and-white overshot coverlet and a stencilled Windsor settle, shine. Other aged pieces crafted in warm woods, such as a four-poster bed, a side table, a bureau, and a trunk, are handsome but unobtrusive, which strikes the right balance in the space.*

RIGHT: *Most authentic country beds don't come in contemporary sizes, but a bit of ingenuity can compensate for this. Here, a vintage wrought-iron garden gate from the turn of the century was made into a headboard for a standard queen-size bed. The bed, coupled with a vividly graphic quilt and a bright green cabinet filled with a collection of vintage sewing boxes, has given this plain white room a quaint countrified personality.*

RIGHT: *The right textiles can make a room. Here, a mix of sweet floral and gingham prints along with a hooked rug add cottage chic to a child's room. The fact that the fabrics are both old and new and are used in unconventional ways (such as for cushions on upholstered pieces and as double-sided valances) makes the mix more interesting.*

ABOVE: *A beautifully detailed bed can make a dramatic statement, whether it is a full-blown four-poster configuration or a sensible metal frame. Here, a painted white brass bed goes from slightly shabby to unabashedly romantic thanks to pristine linens lavishly layered with lace. The flowery wallpaper furthers the mood and adds a dash of sunny color to the room.*

ABOVE: *The informality of a country decor allows for lots of leeway. In this tiny attic bedroom, many distinct and eclectic elements are used to achieve a romantic mood, including a mint-hued balloon shade, intricate floral wallpaper, a painted bureau, and a boldly appliquéd quilt on a fancifully curved bed. Rather than fight for center stage, these devices harmonize thanks to their subtle tones.*

ABOVE: *A subdued green mural of rolling hills makes a relaxing backdrop for a room of rest, and coordinates particularly well with rustic pieces of furniture such as a four-poster bed, a fan-back Windsor chair, a provincial trunk, and oval Shaker boxes.*

ABOVE: *Beautifully carved box beds, which were enclosed on three sides and afforded their occupants privacy and warmth, were common in the European countryside. An "all-American" version is a perfect fit in this small log cabin. Built into a tiny alcove, this box bed accommodates two sleepers and affords lots of storage under each platform, creating a guest room with maximum privacy in a minimal space.*

LEFT, TOP: *A tiny attic guest room becomes an engaging multipurpose spot with careful planning. The sofa is situated on the wall of the room with enough ceiling height to accommodate someone sitting up, while the bed is tucked under the eaves. Painting the wood-paneled sloped ceiling white also opens up the small space. Finally, a patchwork quilt, a metal bed, and a wood chest give the small room its country demeanor.*

LEFT, BOTTOM: *Country style doesn't always call for purism. An ornate French sleigh bed and tailored English pine chest get a dose of pure Americana of the regional sort from an adobe hearth. The simplicity of the setting and a neutral palette help unify the disparate elements and make the room work.*

OPPOSITE: *A four-poster bed so strongly defines country style that its presence can give a contemporary loft the same brand of country ambience as a rough-hewn cabin. Although a few pieces, such as a wood bench and side table, further the country feeling, it is the linens, and especially a length of plain muslin draped horizontally over the frame, that reinforce the mood. This modern interpretation of the traditional canopy is cost-effective, easily installed, and a perfect match with the drapes over the mammoth glass doors in the room.*